THIS IS ME

Written and illustrated by

Mai Sands

The best thing you can do for yourself is to be gentle and kind. Remember that always ♡

Mai Sands ♡

Contents

Acknowledgements

Part 1: Life
Trains
To the people who come and go
I am a stepping stone
Stepping stones
No pieces
Dreams
Angel baby
Shattered smile
The Globe Café
My name is January
By the sea
Books
Henry

Part 2: Love
A story for him
November rain
Jack and Rose
Forever and a day
Goodbyes
The Tree
No mountain or sea
Him
Would you still love me?
Space Robots
Looking for love
Lost love

Part 3: Mental Health
Sat in the dark
Darkness
She is Anxiety

Dear Anxiety
I know I am pretty
Its bad again
The hardest days
The Inevitable Decline
I'm okay
Cells
Red
Scars
Dear Future please be kind

Final Notes

Acknowledgements

I want to thank so many people but if I did this would go on forever and you would never get to read any of my poetry. So, I will keep this as short at possible as it is already way too long.

I want to thank my incredible family and friends; especially my mother Helen for all the support and love they have provided me on this process and the constant encouragement to be creative. You are forever my rock.

I couldn't publish this without thanking Gemma, Ants and The Globe Writers for pushing me in the right direction, supplying me with a warm and welcoming environment to write and grow as a creator and the never-ending support you provided me and the community in all our writing adventures. I'd have not made it this far without you.

Without these glorious people I would have never had the courage to venture out of my comfort zone and take the risk of publishing this deeply personal book.

I love you all. Thank you!

Part 1: Life

"You have brains in your head and feet in your shoes you can steer yourself in any direction you choose."

~ Dr Seuss

Trains

Trains come
Trains go
Living life to and fro
Sometimes here
Sometimes there
Travelling the rails with no fear
Meeting so many people along the way
Changing their lives in so many ways
But one day they will stop
And left to rot
In a graveyard of other trains
All left to be forgot.

To the people who come and go

As time passes by
people come and go
Life's clock ticking
I can't pause time I know
But sometimes I want to stop for just a while
And remind the people that won't stay
That I wish them well on their way
I don't wish they find happiness as strong as fire
It may be warm and bright
But the light will flicker and go out
I wish them Happiness like the air we breathe
Constantly there in the breeze

Or like a river
Twisting and turning
Adapting and flowing
Having no worries
As the river will always find its way back to the sea
No matter how far away it will be
Rushing strong
Soft and steady
Always there when you are ready
Home to animals
keeping them free
Thats how I want their happiness to be.

I am a stepping stone

I am a stepping stone
A halfway point
The stop in time
The breath of fresh air
Who loves and supports and fixes the wounds
With pieces of myself
Then watches you go
And live life wholeheartedly
With love and support and happiness
Which will bring me such joy
And emptiness
As I watch you bloom and grow
Into the new life you create
that would be the life I would choose
If I were not a stepping stone.

Stepping Stones

Who is there for the stepping stones?
Oh, don't you see
When you step and use and take and love
You leave with pieces of me.
But what do I get when you are gone?
When I'm so alone needing support
Knowing I've been forgotten.
Because the stepping stones of life
Are always the fixers
The ones who make life shine
Brighter than the stars in the sky
But even though they try
The emptiness that consumes them
Should be some sort of crime
Because who is there for the stepping stones?
They always end up so alone
Who cares when they want to cry
When they melt to the bedroom floor
Questioning why
Why they never get in return
All the love and support and holes they fix
When they are left with more wounds than you know
Who is there for the stepping stones?

No Pieces

I am a stepping stone
With no pieces left to give
So, stepping in my stepping zone
Would make me crumble
Leaving me with no life to live.

Dreams

Sleeping, Slumbering, Shuddering and shaking
Bed nobs and broomstick beds escaping
Leaping from windows, then slowly waiting
By waves of blue and skies of white
Storms approaching
Turning day to night.
A little sailboat, all on its own
Leaping the waves, disguising someone's home
Swirling whirlpools, sucking them in
Will this be their end, or where they begin?
My bed's long legs leap down, down, down
All the way to the whirlpools eye
Till we are falling through the sky
Flying like Aladdin's carpet
Fingers through clouds
Only us now, nobody's around
Land on the shore in the rolling hills of green
The bed takes us on another adventure
There are new places to be seen
Sunflowers bloom from beneath our feet
Rolling like roller skates through the lush grass below
Where it is taking me, I do not know
Stopping at a house lets me get down
It's a little cosy cabin, made of sweets
Inside the scene isn't so neat
Hand pause on the door handle
Bracing myself, One, Two, Three
A wolf jumps out and eats me
Luckily, though, I'm now back home
No flying beds or fields of green
Just me, my cat and a bizarre dream.

Angel Baby

Tiny fingers
Tiny toes
Tiny hands wrapped around my fingers
Smell of Lavender in the bath
Smell of freshly washed skin
Smell of Talcum Powder in the air.

Tiny outfits oh so small
Wriggling legs
Waving arms
Screeching and crying
Cooing and giggling

Holding one so close
Listening to its soft breath grow slow
Tiny heart beats growing weak
For the baby that was never meant to be.

Shattered Smile

Silent screams suffocating under your love
In the darkness shattered pieces of my heart rise above
Broken promises I'm drowning in the sea of your lies
Bitter tears stain my cheeks as our love finally dies
Tangled knots finding hope among my tear stained cries
Haunted memories echo a painful symphony of goodbyes
A silent whisper of sorrow in my mind
Time stands still as the scars of abuse unwind
Lost in the shadows searching for a love I'll never find
Imprisoned by the past but my soul won't be confined
Yet the pain of its rebellion makes me want to cry
Knowing it hasn't learnt its lesson even though I have tried
With no support system the darkness is where I confide
Feeling It's safety as I attempt to hide
Wondering if this is all I am going to have in life
As I continue to suffocate in love after love
Never to find myself rising above.

The globe Cafe

The Globe Cafe
A place to go and hide away
With a good book
Coffee in hand
The perfect place to go on a rainy day

The globe cafe
Full of fun
Something there for everyone
Writing groups
Book clubs
Poetry slams and more
Everyone is welcome when they walk through that door

The globe Cafe
My favourite place
Memories and friendships line the walls
Of this glorious space
Not just a cafe I'd like to say
But home in so many ways.

My name is January

Hello, my name is January
The less exciting sister
December is the one
Everyone says they miss her
December has the lights, the dazzle, the awe
Where January is hardly spoke about anymore

Hello, my name is January
The less exciting sister
The one everyone says
They wouldn't miss her
As January is dull, quiet and alone
Where December is cosy with the family all home

Hello, my name is January
I am the less exciting sister
December has Christmas
Santa and gifts
January has nothing but memories we miss

Hello, my name is January
I am the less exciting sister
Though I know my branches are bare
And the excitement has disappeared
Please do remember
I can be the start of all your hopes and dreams
For the coming Year.

By the Sea

By the sea
Thats where you will find me
Warm sun rays
Sparkling waves
Golden sand
Toes dug deep
By the sea
That's where you will find me

Sea Gulls squawk
Morning walks
By the sea
That's where you will find me

Cocktails and sunbeds
Beach towels spread out
By the sea
That's where you will find me

A perfect little holiday
Somewhere far, far away
As long as it is by the sea
That's where you will find me.

Books

Books are soul food
Able to push you through a rollercoaster of moods
Magical worlds just for you
Taking you away from the things you have to do
A holiday from life
A slow deep breath
Giving that busy brain a rest
It fills your heart
From the very start
With words so sweet
It tops up your fantasies
Or words so sad
You didn't know you could cry like that
Books are soul food
Available for every mood.

<u>Henry</u>

Little boy all mine
Created with such care
Going through the process
With nobody else there

You are my saviour
In a world where I felt so alone
Just look at us now
How much we have both grown

A boy so sweet
A joy to meet
Constantly teaching me
What love is meant to be

A little boy who is all mine
This poem is your sign
I will love you
Forever and a day
I'll never be too far away.

Part 2: Love

"To love and be loved is to feel the sun

from both sides"

~ David Viscott

A story for him

Sunbeams moonbeams
Lighthouse in the shadows
Soothing voice in the storm
When my sparks almost out

Pretty words and poetry
Sentiments so wonderful
I feel like I'm dreaming
Too good to be true
My head continues screaming

Angel eyes and butterflies
Maps yet to be traced
You were my puzzle piece
But the story is yet to be complete

Confusion and hurt
Is what is left behind
After three months
Giving me a wonderful time
Story book perfect
I could write you a top selling novel
It would be all I have left of you
And yet it wont comfort
The loss you made mine
Sunbeams moonbeams
Angel eyes and dimpled smiles
All but a distant memory
As I hurt for a while.

November Rain

Through the darkness
Sorrow and pain
Comes a moment that is rare these days
A quiet little moment
A swirl of silence
Unexpected and strange
Yet here I sit listening
Watching the world start glistening
Like a lazy November rain

I'm drawn to him
Like a moth to a flame
Fluttering a flitting
Something sitting
Pulling at the corners of my smile
Asking if I can stay a while

I do not dare question
The quiet little moment
Unexpected and strange
Like a lazy Sunday morning
Slow and still
Collecting raindrops on my windowsill.

Jack and Rose

No mountain is high enough
No stars are bright enough
When our love grows
My soul will sing
My heart will fly
Because you're my everything.

Your eyes shine like stars
Your smile lights up the dark
Your beauty captured my heart
But don't you know
I love you like Jack loved his Rose.

Forever and a day

Heart pounds at your smile
Head spins at your laugh
Every minute I mentally beg to last
Forever and a day
So I can love you my way
Life without you
Isn't worth knowing
I'd follow you
Wherever you were going
Is this love?
I think so
Especially from all the things that you show

Your compassion, oh how sweet
Kindness and understanding
For all the needs of mine that you meet
Gentle words and funny actions
Towards all the challenges you greet
Even with the hard times
Your calm cool head
Cuts my anxiety almost dead
I miss you when you aren't around
Even when I don't make a sound
My sweetheart, my lover, my king
You make my soul sing
I will love you
Forever and a day.

Goodbyes

Crushing feelings
On the heart
Knowing you must depart
Goodbyes are so bittersweet
Leaving a gap till we next meet
But the gap is so cold, lonely and dull
Compared to when you are there
My life feels full
Counting the hours, minutes and seconds
Till I get the hug that always beckons.

The Tree

I may be the tree
Standing tall
For all to see
My branches rising high
Into the sky
Growing fruit
And letting it fall
All the beautiful colours
Dancing in the wind
But soon I start to droop
And my branches become bare
The winds may hit
But never fear
For he is my roots
Staying strong and firm
Deep in the ground
Keeping me upright
When the weather gets bad
He supplies me with food and water
Helping me grow
Then eventually the colours sprout
And fruits grow
But the tree couldn't do it without the roots
A united team that will never end
Forever and ever
till the end of time.

No mountain or sea

No mountain or sea
Could keep you from me
No moon or star
Could ever compete
With the beauty
Of the kaleidoscope of emotions
And the twinkle in your eyes
And every thundering heart beat
Making me realise
Life is too short
To be afraid of pain
When there is so much to gain
In your embrace, your touch, your smile, your scent
With the only intent
To experience, explore and feel
Debate if it's real
You have captured my brain
The thought of you driving me insane
No need to explain
The emotions I feel
Because you make them feel so real
No longer need to hide
Because you make me happy inside
No mountain or sea
would keep you from me
Because don't you see
You mean everything to me.

Him

Skin on fire
Full of desire
Heart so full
So much to give
How I want to live
In your embrace
Settle in the delicacies
You have in place
Three little words
settle in our eyes
Yet no words will be said
Only to linger in our head
Wishes and wants
Follow us to bed
All insecurities fall dead
When eyes meet
And hands greet
It feels like a fairy story.

Would you still love me?

Would you still love me
When I'm wrinkled and old?
when my hair thins out
When you go bald

Would you still love me
If I was a worm
wriggling in dirt
Making it my home

Would you still love me
If I could not speak
Having to learn sign language
For weeks and weeks

Would you still love me
If I was a frog
Living my best life
In a dirty old bog

Would you still love me
At the end of time
When there isn't a soul left
Would you still be mine

Space Robots

Love letters
Lullabies
Never having to say goodbyes
Counting the stars in the sky
Forever standing by your side

It will always start with this
A simple good morning kiss
It will be something I always miss

Serenade me to sleep
Beautiful dreams I wish to keep
Tell me a story
We will laugh all night
Till the morning is already shining bright
Through my too thin curtains
This only makes me even more certain
I will love you lots and lots
Like super space robots.

Looking for love

We were looking for love
Looking at the same stars
Reading the same books
Hoping for someone out there to love us
To start a home, a family
Something so simple yet so happy
Magic sparking in just one kiss
I know we both wished for this
A lifetime awaits
Starting from that fateful day
When all our wishes came true
The day when I met you.

Love Lost

I don't love you anymore
And that is it
The end of the story
Nothing left in this for me
All that I feel
Is a numbness so real
I don't love you anymore

I know those words hurt
But I'm not sorry
I know this is all because of me
That is how it must be
But I don't love you anymore

I really don't want this to end
But I can never predict
What is round the bends
Our whole lives together
Will stay a dream forever
Because I don't love you anymore.

Part 3: Mental Health

" Mental pain is less dramatic than physical pain, but it is more common and also harder to bear. The frequent attempt to conceal mental pain increases the burden: it is easier to say 'My tooth is aching' than to say 'My heart is broken.' "

~ C.S. Lewis

Trigger warning!

The next section involves triggering subjects such as body image issues, depression, suicidal thoughts and self-harm.

Read at your own discretion.

Sat in the dark

I'm sat in the dark
Wondering where I am in my life's ark
Wondering if life is as beautiful as
All the poets and painters and story makers believe

I'm sat in the dark
With the weight of the world
Balancing life like it's my only goal
Hoping things won't be so heavy

As I sink further down
Into this pit of quicksand
Ready to eat any happiness, I find
Any positive thoughts
Any plans for life
Leaving me empty inside

With no purpose
Just living the life I was created to walk
With curve balls, torture, tears and hate
Nothing to stop me from being late
To my own funeral

Am I too late to escape the box I put myself in
The category I don't feel like I fit in
The ache inside as I try to find
My purpose for living
The reason to open my eyes

To find my people while blind in the dark
Scrambling around like I have a plan
Setting an example for future generations
When really, I'm winging every step, I take

Questioning every decision I make
Wondering what effect I will have on a world full of hate

Yet somehow, I appear like I've got everything together
A house, A child, A Husband, A business
The literal image of a perfect life
And yet I'm drowning in my own strife
Suffocating in pressure to perform the way society expects
No wriggle room for the quirky and kind
Just perfect, prim and proper
The embodiment of professional

Mental health is a term the young people use
Us adults are too old to use such terms you see
we are meant to have it together already
"Nothing wrong with me"

Silent screaming inside my head
The child is dying inside my heart
The constant pressure making it hard to breathe
Reminding me that I really am crazy.

Darkness

My compass that once led me to you
Is spiralling in all directions
Leaving me unsure what to do
Like in the middle of a storm
Wind wrapping round me
Unable to look up
And see the eye
The peace in the centre
Leaving me so focused on the closed door
I want to enter
I forget about the window that's open

Blessings are near they say
So why can't I feel them
Christmas is here they say
But not for me today
No jolly, no joy, no angels singing
Just me in my bedroom
Trying to find something to believe in
No god has helped, no prayers have been answered
No sign or directions
Just never ending emptiness
When will this darkness end?
Where is the light?
I'm so tired of living in the night.

She is Anxiety

Me and my anxiety
Are in an abusive relationship
Constantly fighting
Slapping and shouting
Weeds only sprouting
She dresses in a sun dress
Twirling in the sun
Seeming so sweet
Yet really, she is the devil
I willingly greet
Slipping into her shadows
Trying to make myself at home
Dreading the moments we are left alone
Knowing the shouting and screaming
Slapping and bleeding
Is all that she is needing from me
She laughs while I cry
Smiling while I die
She is the mask I wear outside
But secretly I sit
Inside her shell
Knowing if I don't wrestle my way out
I will never become well
So I fight and I fight
Every day
Just to keep her at bay.

Dear Anxiety

Dear Anxiety,
Stop and listen to me please
I promise the thoughts
Rattling around inside our head are not real
So kill them dead
I promise it's okay
To ask for help
No body is going to yell
I promise we are okay
To laugh and sing and be happy
I promise we aren't going daffy
I know this is all hard to hear
That you have believed this
Year after year
But I promise, even though we feel like dying
That your mind is lying
That happiness is within our reach
You just need to spread your hand out
And grasp it
I promise above everything else
You don't need to be afraid
I promise you everything will be okay
You are loved, liked, cared for
So maybe it's time to shut the door?
On all that pain and darkness, we carry
To let in some of the laughter and light
And maybe then we will sleep peacefully tonight.

I Know I Am Pretty

I know I am pretty
Mum, you tell me everyday
I know that I am Pretty
But I don't feel that way
I look at my hair and wish
I could style it like that girl
I saw in my class
Or apply make up
Like the models in movies and TV
Or to become thin
But not too much
And not gain too much weight that people will watch
I want a perfect smile
But I know that life hasn't been kind
And things in life
Have prevented that from being mine
I know that I am pretty Mum
You tell me every day
But why then can't I see it that way?
Why do I feel like an imposter in my own skin
No matter what I do I will never win
No matter what clothes I wear
Or how I style my hair
I will never be as pretty
As the other girls out there.

It's Bad Again

I know it's got bad again
When death feels more welcoming
Than my own home

I know it's bad again
When I can feel the pain
From memories far far away

I know it's bad again
When the covers feel like a thousand pounds
Weighing me down into the bed
Keeping me from saying the words that need to be said

I know it's got bad again
when life seems to be spinning
Too fast to see
Leaving me feeling constantly dizzy

I know it's got bad again
When food feels like razers
Slashing my throat as it goes down

I know it's bad again
When I feel like I'm drowning
In my own blood that runs round my body
Slashing my skin
Just to feel something

I know it's bad again
When I just want to cry
Wishing I could curl up and die.

The hardest days

I passed my hardest days alone
And that is okay
Nobody knew it anyway
Just because I wear depression so well
Like a jacket made of gold
Sparkling in the sun
Making sure there is a smile for everyone
Doesn't mean I don't find it heavy
That my knees want to buckle under the weight
That secretly I do hate
The way it shines
Through my fake smile
How it kills the twinkle in my eyes
Creating more pain inside

Just because I wear anxiety's dress with unwanted pride
Doesn't mean I don't silently cry
In the bathrooms of public spaces
Trying to convince myself that this place
Is safe and secure and warm and happy
Even though I feel so crappy
I lived through the hardest days alone
So I could now build a place I can call home
So I could make friends and laugh, sing and love
To enjoy everything life brings
Even when days are hard
Nothing was as bad as the stuff at the start.

The Inevitable Decline

What goes up must
Must come down
The inevitable decline
Gravity showing us
That science is all around
What goes up must come down
The inevitable decline

What goes up
Must come down
The inevitable decline
Even if you are on cloud nine
See this as your sign
What goes up must come down
The inevitable decline

What goes up
Must come down
The inevitable decline
like a paper plane
flying through the sky
No matter how streamlined
What goes up must come down
The inevitable decline.

I'm Okay

Don't ask me if I'm okay
The answer will always be yes
Even when my head is swimming
In a vat of depressive poison
Making me wish I didn't exist

Don't ask if I am okay
The answer will always be yes
Even when I plaster on a smile
To hide the screaming inside my soul
Clawing at my insides trying to get out
But I laugh in an attempt to forget what I'm sad about

Don't ask me if I'm okay
The answer will always be yes
Even when my skin feels too tight across my bones
And every movement feels like torture
It's at least a place that starts to feel like home

Don't ask if I'm okay
The answer will always be yes
Because to admit that I'm struggling
Will lead to my death.

Cells

Cells
Is that really where I'm meant to be?
A cosy padded room
Made just for me
Do I really appear that crazy?

Is it too late to start again?
To listen to the therapist
When she says I'm unwell
To take the never-ending pills
The drugged happy
Is better than this apparently
A fake smile over real joy
Is that really all life is?

Am I so easily discarded?
Locked away and forget where this all started...
A little girl, afraid and alone
With nowhere to really call home

Does she really deserve that room?
To rot away within her own doom
Even the gloom looks happier than she would be
How am I the only one that can see clearly
The damage you are doing
By calling me crazy.

<u>Red</u>

Red...
It has become my friend
Warm and welcoming
Calming and smooth
Stopping the never-ending buzzing
The shaking and tugging
The screaming and crying
Its all okay now
Red is here

My own personal hero
Ready at a moment's notice
Calms me and allows me to focus
Deep breath in
Deep breath out
I no longer need to shout
Just one more time
And I think I'll be fine
Because Red is here.

Scars

Scars may scatter my skin
But they will never compare
To the ones littered within
The ones on the outside get to heal
Leaving a mark so I know that it's real
Those that sit inside my head
The ones that scream
I'm better off dead
Those are the ones who permanently bleed
Tainting every good deed
With doubt and insecurity
Never letting me fully believe
That I am able to be happy, loved and liked
That one day I will sleep soundly at night
It fills me with dread when I'm already tired
Bleeds into everything
Never staying quiet
Those are the scars you don't get to see
Those are the wounds I have to fight constantly.

Dear future please be kind

Dear future please be kind
I know the last few years
Will be something I want to erase from my mind
But please if you hear my plea
Just take a second to think of me
Spot all the hard work
The good deeds
The patience and sacrifice
Recognise all the people, I was nice to
That didn't deserve kindness or compassion
All the moments I stopped and begged
For a better morning, A better end
For all the people who became my friend
All the restless nights and work with no breaks
All the appointments and pills
Never ending bills
All the times I stopped to cry
And question why
For all the love I spread about
For all the times I didn't shout
For all the moments I wanted to give up but didn't
For all the people I am yet to meet
I'm begging you
Dear future... Please
Be kind.

Final notes

Thats all folks! thank you so much for reading. The adventure was a long one spanning from the age of 16 all the way through to 26 years old. It was a rollercoaster of laughs, tears, many many therapy appointments but most of all piles and piles of love.

As you can see throughout, I faced some clear challenges, luckily, I didn't have to face them completely alone. If you ever feel like you or someone you know is struggling, I will provide you with some UK services you can contact. you never have to face the battle of mental health alone! There are people out there that care.

And just so you know.... **The Future was kind.**

Samaritans: 24 hours, 365 days a year. you can call free on: **116 123.**

SANline: if you are experiencing mental health problems or supporting someone who is: **0300 304 7000** (4:30pm-10pm everyday)

National suicide prevention help line: **0800 689 5652** (6pm-12am everyday)

CALM: **0800 58 58 58**

SHOUT: A 24-hour text service that is completely free. Text: **85258**

If you feel you are in crisis and need urgent help do not hesitate to reach out to your local mental health services. If you are in danger, please call 999.

Printed in Great Britain
by Amazon